The Three Dimensions
of Freedom

Billy Bragg

The Three Dimensions of Freedom

FABER & FABER

First published in the UK and US in 2019
by Faber & Faber Ltd
Bloomsbury House, 74–77 Great Russell Street,
London, WC1B 3DA

Typeset by Faber & Faber Ltd
Printed and bound by CPI Group (UK) Ltd, Croydon, CR0 4YY

A CIP record for this book
is available from the British Library

ISBN 978–0–571–35321–7

2 4 6 8 10 9 7 5 3

When you're a star, they let you do it.
You can do anything.

—Donald Trump

If one meets a powerful person, ask
them five questions: 'What power have
you got? Where did you get it from? In
whose interests do you exercise it? To
whom are you accountable? And how
can we get rid of you?'

—Tony Benn

Introduction

Human beings have never had so much power. Technology has delivered into our hands the ability to talk across continents and see our contact as we do it, to summon myriad points of information at the touch of a screen. It has given us a platform from which to broadcast our opinions. The promise that the world can be tailored to your demands – providing you're happy to surrender your personal details and preferences – is the new social contract.

Freedom has been repackaged as the right to choose, but genuine choice – in housing, in the workplace, at the ballot box – is hard to come by. While capitalism has delivered a surfeit of connectivity, the past decades have seen a diminution of the individual's ability to exercise control over their economic situation. This lack of agency has led to the wave of populist anger that is spreading across Western democracies. Voters who could once be relied upon to support moderate policies are fired up with the notion of 'taking back control'.

When progress is swift, the changes unleashed can be destructive as well as emancipatory. 'Disruption' may be a buzzword for tech start-ups, but for those in low-paid work it has a more threatening implication. While technology has liberated debate, taking the national conversation out of the hands of gatekeepers, it has also encouraged polarisation.

Our liberty to express ourselves on social media 24/7 has given us a perception of freedom, but if we hope to escape from the partisan climate in which belligerence is never far from the surface, we must first recognise that liberty provides a one-dimensional notion of freedom.

The ability to say whatever you think, to whomever you want, whenever you choose, without any regard for truth or accountability does not guarantee that an individual is free. If it did, Donald Trump would be freedom's shining paragon. While many may use the terms interchangeably, the president's Twitter feed is a daily reminder that liberty and freedom are not the same thing.

Liberty is cherished because it empowers us to think, speak and act as we wish, providing the foundation of freedom. However, further dimensions are required to secure that right for the many and to protect it from the powerful. If your liberty is to be more than just a form of privilege, you must recognise and uphold the right of everyone else to think, speak and act as they wish. Without equal respect for the rights of others, liberty becomes nothing more than licence.

Equality provides a second dimension to freedom by requiring the individual to reciprocate the rights that they claim for themselves.

However, just as free speech alone is not sufficient to define freedom, neither does equality guarantee that an individual has agency over their situation. History has shown that emancipation can be followed by circumstances that declare communities to be equal but separate, the newly liberated falling victim to a campaign of deliberate marginalisation.

If we are to be truly free, then liberty and equality need to be enhanced by the addition of a third dimension: accountability. Whereas liberty empowers the individual and equality requires reciprocity, accountability combines both characteristics to create an environment in which freedom is no longer divorced from responsibility.

This third dimension is crucial if we are seeking to engender agency. Liberty gives freedom its focus, equality its scope, but accountability gives freedom its teeth. Morality, having proved an inadequate means of curbing avaricious bankers and dishonest presidents, no longer has the capacity to protect the weak from the strong. Shame has ceased to sting the powerful. Accountability provides us with a fulcrum with which to recalibrate the balance of power.

Over the past five decades, the globalisation of the world economy has weakened the power of regulatory democracy. As a result, immense wealth has been showered on those individuals working in the financial sector, while many in the real economy have faced inequality and exclusion.

Corporations have captured the democratic process, making it increasingly difficult for citizens to vote for reforms that will make the economy work for everyone. Electoral systems deliver results that do not reflect the popular vote; gerrymandering favours incumbent parties; big money twists opinion. And as artificial intelligence plays a greater role in our lives, decisions made by algorithms are raising the question of where accountability lies in the digital sphere.

People are angry. Neoliberalism has proved unable to deliver the standard of living their parents enjoyed in the post-war years: the security of a decent wage; a job for life; an affordable home; and the sense of a bright future. Is it any surprise that, when offered more of the same free market solutions, voters opt for a guy who simply promises to make things great again?

Authoritarianism is on the rise. Demagogues deploy the term 'fake news' to both create division and deflect criticism. In the febrile atmosphere that infects so much online discourse, opinion trumps fact and truth is little more than your perspective on any given day. As a result, freedom has become untethered from its function as a universal principle that protects the individual, and is instead claimed as a fig leaf by those seeking licence to dissemble and abuse.

The key to tackling these problems is accountability: firstly, as a means of restoring agency to the individual; secondly, as the antidote to the power of authoritarians and algorithms.

We live in an age of rage. People feel their voices are ignored by distant elites no longer willing to answer for their actions. This hasn't happened by accident. It is the culmination of a decades-long rearguard action to neuter democracy and marginalise those demanding the three dimensions of freedom: liberty, equality and accountability.

1. LIBERTY

I hear people say we have to stop and debate globalisation. You might as well debate whether autumn should follow summer.

—Tony Blair

What do life, liberty and the pursuit of happiness have in common? The obvious answer is that they are all identified as inalienable rights in the United States Declaration of Independence. Yet it is also true that, despite being universally understood concepts, there is no single definition for what constitutes the condition of any one of them. Even more ironic, then, that the Founding Fathers yoked these ideas together as a means of evoking another notion for which we have never had a good definition: freedom.

To the ancient Greeks, freedom meant escape from bondage; in the twentieth century, it was expressed through the right to vote; today, it is sold to us as the pleasure of driving a new-model car at high speed on a winding mountain road. Time has expanded its scope, as each new generation struggles against the axioms of its elders to establish an idea of being free that reflects its own values.

At its most benign, freedom evokes emancipation; at its most dangerous, impunity. For freedom has myriad manifestations, each reliant on circumstance and perspective. In our attempts to capture the most perfect sense of being free, we are apt to use the metaphor 'as free as a bird', yet the freedom of the bird to feed is incompatible with that of the farmer to grow crops.

The common thread that runs through these competing notions of freedom is the human desire for agency. For much of history, agency was a manifestation of wealth. The contested liberties of first kings and courtiers, then Lords and Commons, led to the development of pluralist democracy, offering a degree of collective agency to all levels of society. For all its frustrations and failings, the democratic model offers us a paradigm of freedom to which many subscribe.

However, democracy's relationship to agency is paradoxical. It evolved both to enhance the right of the individual to control their own destiny and to place limits upon their ability to control that of others. The key to a cohesive society is the balance between agency and compulsion, and a consensus about where that balance lies.

Over the past four decades, economic developments have made such a consensus much harder to achieve. Since the end of the Cold War, the ideology of neoliberalism – a belief that the free market is the best mechanism for distributing resources around society – has come to dominate Western polity. Governments of both left and right have accepted the neoliberal agenda of tax cuts, deregulation, privatisation and hostility to unions.

Neoliberalism is the engine of globalisation, the creation of a single marketplace that recognises neither the borders nor the sovereignty of nations in its pursuit of profit. The ability of goods and services to move between countries without hindrance has lowered prices for the consumer. However, globalisation has also facilitated the movement of jobs, profits and people between states and continents, allowing corporations to circumvent government jurisdiction.

As a result, the individual has little control over their predicament. The power of the unions to bargain for wages and conditions is restricted; the provision of free health care, affordable housing and decent education has been undermined by the profit motive; and the neoliberal determination to both cut taxes *and* balance the books has led to the imposition of austerity.

The ability of democracy to reverse the policies that led to this situation is everywhere trumped by the power of the markets. Having traded their sovereignty for the abundance promised by globalisation, governments of all stripes have little choice but to bend to the neoliberal agenda. Since the financial crash of 2008, people have been desperate for change, yet the system just offers more of the same.

This lack of agency has led to a wave of anger. In an attempt to regain some control over their lives, voters have turned to populist politicians who promise to stem the tide of globalisation by reinforcing national identity.

Yet look beyond the rhetoric of populist leaders and you'll find that they have no intention of challenging the neoliberal agenda. Instead, by reasserting the sovereignty of the nation state, they aim to make globalisation work on their own terms. For all that they seek to overturn the distant elite, they remain determined to keep intact the system that created it.

If their hollow promise of taking back control is not to undermine their support, the populists need to provide some sense of agency to those for whom the pace of modernity has delivered little but economic insecurity. In the early 1990s, the term 'culture war' entered the vocabulary of politics, denoting a polarisation between those who hold traditional values and their fellow citizens who express progressive views.

Many living outside of the major cities in Western democracies feel banished to the periphery of culture, their concerns no longer reflected in mainstream society. While they may not be on the breadline, they are concerned for their status in a swiftly changing world. As a result, their insecurities become less tangible – they worry about patriotism, gender roles, ethnicity, inclusivity. These issues become the front lines in the culture war.

Supporters of corporate power will always be happy to champion cultural supremacy over economic security because it doesn't cost them anything, keeps workers divided, and makes free market cheerleaders in the commentariat sound as if they're on the side of the average joe. Citizens who no longer feel their voices are being heard are encouraged to believe that their vocal resistance to small increments of social change is proof of their agency.

Superficially, the notion of a culture war seems trivialised into arguments about whether or not Christians are allowed to say 'Merry Christmas' rather than the more inclusive 'Happy Holidays'. While this may not be an issue of substance to the disinterested observer, the loudly expressed taking of offence over trivial matters is a key aspect of the campaign against political correctness. The inversion of virtue signalling, it is a performative prejudice that relies on inflating the meaning of minor incidents out of all proportion to their actual significance.

For those unable to control the economic

changes that are making their lives more inse-cure, a culture war provides an outlet for their rage. And for the politicians who exploit it, the campaign against political correctness ensures that rage is discharged against minorities rather than at the system that oppresses them.

When, during the first Republican Party presidential debate in 2015, Donald Trump was challenged over disrespectful comments he had made about women, he brushed aside the ques-tion with a declaration of cultural warfare. 'I think the big problem this country has is being politically correct. I've been challenged by so many people, and I don't frankly have time for total political correctness. And to be honest with you, this country doesn't have time either.'

Trump's ability to dismiss charges of impro-priety with ease – and to shrug off all criticism for doing so – sent a message to everyone who felt that the advancement of women, people of colour and the young had been at their personal cost, and who was sick of being told that they had to be polite about it.

Resistance to being coerced into accepting cultural change became the rallying cry of Trump's campaign. Where other politicians took a dog-whistle approach to hot-button issues like race, gender, immigration and climate change, Trump used a bullhorn to dismiss his enemies, humiliate progressives and open old wounds in American society. The blows he landed were below the belt, but his crowd loved the spectacle. It was raucous, transgressive fun, mostly at the expense of the coastal elites. And, after years of being looked down upon by mainstream culture, it felt like winning.

The people who put Trump into the White House are not losers, but they do feel under threat – from many of the things that he attacked in his campaign. But does that which he declared to be the biggest threat of all – political correctness – really exist? After all, it has no ideology, nor philosophical doctrine setting out its aims. No political party promises to implement it and no one marches in protest waving banners demanding it.

Although political correctness seems very real to those citizens who are troubled by it, it is largely a projection of their own powerlessness. Like the monster lurking under the bed when Mummy turns out the light, political correctness is the sum of their insecurities. If we hope to challenge this knee-jerk hostility to progressive ideas, we first need to understand where those insecurities come from.

In 1960, the economic theorist Friedrich Hayek published *The Constitution of Liberty*, in which he argued that the greatest threat to freedom was the regulation of markets. Its opening line reads: 'We are concerned in this book with that condition of men in which coercion of some by others is reduced as much as is possible in society.' For Hayek, the expectation that each individual should contribute to the collective provision of social services according to their means was a form of coercion.

Born in Vienna in 1889, Hayek came to Britain in 1931 to teach at the London School of Economics. He was a supporter of the Austrian School of economic thought, which held that no action should be taken during times of economic crisis to prevent the collapse of companies no longer able to sustain their viability. Hayek saw freedom as an expression of the personal desires of individuals, as manifested by the workings of the market. Agency was achieved by the prices they accepted in their choices as consumers and sellers.

Seemingly unconcerned about the accumulation of wealth, Hayek focused his criticism on government efforts to tackle inequality through the redistribution of resources. His ideas had a huge influence on Margaret Thatcher and Ronald Reagan, providing the philosophy that underpins neoliberalism. While at the LSE, Hayek was a colleague of John Maynard Keynes, the most influential economist of his day, whose theories were challenging the wisdom of the market that had held sway since the eighteenth century.

As a system driven by competition, the free market has no need of equality and, in place of accountability, it relies on an invisible hand. That was the metaphor used by Adam Smith to describe the way in which unintended economic benefits could arise from the self-interested decisions of individuals acting freely within a market. Smith articulated this theory in *The Wealth of Nations*, published in 1776, which provides the theological basis for those who believe that the free market offers the best method for distributing resources within society. If left to regulate itself, they argue, the market will naturally find an equilibrium which delivers benefits to all.

However, Adam Smith was a moralist as well as an economist. In his earlier work, *The Theory of Moral Sentiments* (1759), he warned against the dangers of untrammelled self-interest. Competition, rather than freedom from regulation, is the crucial element that makes the invisible hand function and, as Smith realised, wherever there is competition, there need to be rules and referees to ensure that cheats do not prosper at the expense of others.

During the Great Depression of the 1930s, economists were made painfully aware that the free market economy had no automatic mechanism for recovery. The invisible hand had failed. In response to the economic crisis, John Maynard Keynes argued that, as consumers drove growth in the modern economy, governments needed to borrow during times of financial insecurity in order to fund the construction of public works. Such projects would put money in the pockets of ordinary workers, who would in turn spend their wages in the real economy, restoring confidence.

In advocating government intervention, Keynes rejected the laissez-faire economics that had predominated since the early nineteenth century, instead offering democracy a greater element of regulation over the free market. The 1945 Labour government followed his prescriptions, instituting a social democratic programme that provided free health care and decent housing. Legislation strengthened workers' rights, improving conditions and bargaining power in the workplace. Labour nationalised the public utilities, along with the mines, railways and docks. Adam Smith's invisible hand was replaced with the nurturing hand of the welfare state.

These radical policies were not reversed when the Conservatives gained power in 1951, leading commentators to speak of a post-war consensus around the idea of the state providing support for the individual from the cradle to the grave. By 1957, the mixture of Keynesian economics, redistributive taxation and welfare provision had brought about such improvement in the standard of living that Conservative prime minister Harold Macmillan was moved to remark that the British people had 'never had it so good'.

This post-war prosperity was not confined to the UK. By adopting Keynesian economic policies to varying degrees, the US, France, Italy, Germany and Japan all achieved record growth and low unemployment. The gap between rich and poor began to narrow. There was still poverty to be seen, but the onus was now on the state to provide, rather than on individuals to fend for themselves.

Social democracy had brought capitalism to heel. A mixed economy of private and public ownership, regulated markets and free collective bargaining in the workplace had created an economy that worked for the benefit of the majority.

However, not everybody was happy with this state of affairs.

While none of them wanted to go back to the bad old days of the 1930s, there were many industrialists and financiers who chafed at the restrictions imposed by Keynesian economics. When they couldn't even rely on their old pals in the Conservative Party to stand up for the idea of free markets, they realised that they could no longer control the economy in the way they had done before universal suffrage, when the rich made laws for their own benefit.

Accountability had shifted the balance of power in favour of the masses. If they hoped to regain their dominance, the rich would have to break the monopoly that democracy held over policymaking.

In 1947, a group of libertarian economists gathered in the Swiss village of Mont Pelerin to discuss how to combat the statist economics that were sweeping Western democracies. The conference was organised by Friedrich Hayek.

For those attending this foundational meeting of the Mont Pelerin Society, the mixed economies of the Western democracies were just as pernicious as the command economies of the totalitarian Marxist states. 'Over large stretches of the Earth's surface the essential conditions of human dignity and freedom have already disappeared,' began their Statement of Aims. 'In others they are under constant menace from the development of current tendencies of policy.' For 'current tendencies' read social democracy.

Hayek and his confederates pledged to take up the cause of economic freedom, to rekindle the notion of liberty as freedom from regulation, harnessing the power of the free market to liberate the people from the tyranny of state provision. Given the primacy of Keynesian economics, they believed that it would take at least a generation before their ideas gained traction. To that end, the members of the Mont Pelerin Society spread out across the globe to seek rich backers willing to fund free market think tanks.

In the decades that followed, corporate-backed lobbying groups began arguing in favour of deregulation. The Hoover Institution, the American Enterprise Institute and the Heritage Foundation worked closely together, coordinating their campaigns, a strategy underscored by the fact that their respective boards of directors often comprised the same group of individuals. In the UK, the Institute of Economic Affairs was set up and funded by a member of the Mont Pelerin Society, while Margaret Thatcher was among the founders of the Centre for Policy Studies.

Legend holds that, shortly after she became leader of the Conservative Party, Thatcher attended a briefing at which the speaker suggested the Tories should seek a pragmatic middle way with regard to economic policy. Thatcher didn't wait for him to finish. Reaching into her handbag, she pulled out a copy of *The Constitution of Liberty*, holding it up for all to see. 'This,' she said sternly, 'is what we believe in,' and she slammed Hayek's book down onto the table.

With Thatcher's election in 1979 and that of

Ronald Reagan eighteen months later, Hayek and his followers finally had the opportunity to put their ideas to the test.

Initially, they had no name for their big-business/small-government ideology. Some called it classic liberalism, but the term 'liberal' held different meanings on either side of the Atlantic. A few of the think tanks referred to themselves as libertarian, but most saw that as descriptive of a social rather than an economic position. In a book entitled *Why I Am Not a Conservative*, Hayek himself claimed to be an Old Whig.

For the new breed of financiers who were making fortunes from the Hayekian assault on the post-war consensus, 'Old Whiggery' didn't quite match up to their self-image as buccaneering heroes come to liberate the economy. Over time, they came to be known as neoliberals. They were 'neo' because of their significant break with the past: whereas classic liberalism had been founded on trade in goods between nations, the driving force of neoliberalism is finance and globalisation.

Keynes had recognised that the nation state –
as the largest functioning democratic entity – was
crucial to economic agency, not just as a gener-
ator of GDP but also as a pool from which taxes
could be levied. While trade was to be encouraged, speculative cross-border finance, which had
helped cause the Great Depression, should be
tightly regulated. 'Let goods be homespun whenever it is reasonably and conveniently possible,'
Keynes wrote. 'Above all, let finance be primarily
national.'

By the 1970s, technological advances in communications and transportation were putting
a huge strain on this notion. Manufacturers in
Western Europe and North America began
moving production overseas, where wages were
cheaper and unions non-existent. Democratic
oversight of the financial sector was also break-
ing down. One of the first acts of the Thatcher
government was to remove the exchange controls
that Labour had introduced in 1947 to tightly
regulate overseas capital transactions made by
British citizens.

It was a move that created a decisive change in the balance of power between labour and capital. The option to move to another country if wage bills were judged to be too high was now an attractive prospect to British businesses. This sudden change in policy also put pressure on the working practices of the City of London. Although the bowler hats had mostly vanished by the late 1970s, the atmosphere of an old boys' club still permeated the London stock market. The removal of exchange controls made the idea of face-to-face stockbroking an anachronism.

Thatcher's economic revolution took a great leap forward in 1986, when the City of London was deregulated overnight in what became known as the 'Big Bang'. These changes severely undermined the ability of the state to intervene in the economy. If a future government sought to introduce Keynesian policies, capital could now flee overseas.

The effects of Thatcher's decision to deregulate the economy were devastating. During her first term in office, 25 per cent of British manufacturing was lost. Reform of company law gave primacy to the interests of shareholders, leading to a huge shift in the way profits were distributed. Whereas, in the 1970s, companies remitted an average of 10 per cent of their profits to shareholders, by 2010 the figure was over 60 per cent.

Thatcher's attack on social democracy was mirrored in the US by the policies of President Reagan. Both believed that the free market could solve society's problems, if only it were unshackled from regulation.

During the long years of the post-war consensus, the nascent neoliberals had little to comfort them in terms of popular culture. No pop bands were extolling the virtues of monetarism; few students had a poster of Fritz Hayek on their walls. Yet there was one voice willing to imagine a brave new world: Ayn Rand. The Russian-born novelist had emigrated to the US in 1926; her book *Atlas Shrugged*, published in 1957, is a sci-fi vision of a land governed by naked self-interest.

The plot revolves around a massive sulk by entrepreneurs, who are so upset by red tape that they hide in a valley and refuse to make any new things until the masses are nice to them. The book's hero, a free market freedom fighter heroically resisting the tyranny of regulation, became a role model for neoliberals.

In 1987, a member of Ayn Rand's inner circle was given the second-most powerful job in the US. Alan Greenspan had read *Atlas Shrugged* while it was being written in the 1950s. Thirty years after its publication, Ronald Reagan made him Chair of the Federal Reserve, a post he held until 2006.

Shortly after he left office, Greenspan was asked by a Swiss journalist which candidate he would be supporting in the 2008 presidential elections. His response was revealing. It didn't much matter how he voted, Greenspan replied, because 'we are fortunate that, thanks to globalisation, policy decisions in the US have largely been replaced by global market forces. National security aside, it hardly makes any difference who will be the next president. The world is governed by market forces.'

Hayek's dream was complete. Liberty had been redefined as freedom from economic restraint. Yet no one voted for this outcome. No politician stood for office on the platform of ceding power to the markets. Like the invisible hand that goes about its work unseen and disinterested, globalisation was portrayed as the natural evolution of the laws of supply and demand.

An intangible force working towards the best of all possible outcomes, the global free market took on the characteristics of a deity to those who worshipped at its altar. However, events have shown that capitalism loses all sense of moderation when belief in the power of the markets enters the realm of faith.

The British construction company Carillion offers us a sobering recent example of what can happen when corporations believe that they are simply too big to fail. With 450 UK government contracts to provide services from school dinners to hospital cleaning and prison maintenance, the board of directors felt confident that the government would always bail them out.

This assumption was based partly on the importance of the services that Carillion provided, but there was also a sense that, because the British government was committed to the idea that the private sector always provides better value for money than the public sector, it had a strong ideological imperative to ensure that the company was seen to succeed.

This neoliberal article of faith was shattered when the company collapsed in 2018.

A parliamentary report subsequently found that the directors had prioritised senior executive bonus payouts and shareholder dividends while failing to properly fund the staff pension scheme. Between 2012 and 2016, Carillion paid out £217 million more in dividends than it generated in cash from its operations, suggesting that the company had borrowed money not for investment, but simply to reward shareholders.

The collapse was a complete failure of accountability. The report found that the directors were guilty of 'recklessness, hubris and greed'; the auditors were described as 'complicit' and the regulators as 'too timid to make effective use of the powers they have'. Successive governments were chastised for seeking to outsource work on the cheap.

This was an indictment of what happens when you replace democratic oversight with the profit motive. Having been promised that privatisation would save them money, taxpayers were left to clear up the mess.

The notion that it is possible to have both low taxation and good public services is another central tenet of neoliberal belief. This counter-intuitive idea is often peddled by politicians as a manifesto promise. Yet everyone knows that taxes pay for public services, so if you reduce one, surely the other will suffer?

Not if you can get someone else to pay.

Private finance initiative (PFI) contracts, whereby private companies fund the building and maintenance of national infrastructure, with the government undertaking to pay them back over twenty-five to thirty years, are a sleight of hand designed to give the taxpayer the impression of value for money.

Labour and Conservative governments were attracted to PFI schemes because these made it possible to build new schools and hospitals without having to raise the money up front. PFIs remove public borrowing from the books, reducing the amount of debt the country appears to have. They also have the attraction of making someone else accountable when projects are not delivered on time.

However, these short-term arguments are undermined when interest payments and other incentives are taken into account. By 2019, the private sector had spent an estimated £59.1 billion creating over 700 PFI schemes in the UK, yet, under the current deals, taxpayers will end up paying more than £300 billion for them.

'Trickle-down economics' became a popular slogan around the time of the Reagan presidency. Rather than relying on state intervention to create a fair society, neoliberals argue that taxes on big corporations and the wealthy should be reduced so as to encourage investment, which in turn will lead to more jobs for more people, causing wealth to 'trickle down' throughout society.

This is based on the misconception that only entrepreneurs can create growth. Reward them, and their generosity and acumen will benefit everyone – so the argument goes. However, in terms of value to the real economy, the spending habits of the opulent few are far outweighed by those of the many regular consumers. The individual actions of millions of ordinary people, buying a massive volume of goods and services every day, keeps the economy turning over.

If neoliberals really wanted to encourage growth, they should be calling for the things that would boost consumer confidence: job security, affordable housing and free health care, to name a few.

By 1992, the social democratic policies that were designed to deliver just such resources had been superseded by politicians espousing Third Way politics that they hoped would appeal to voters of both left and right. As a way of justifying his focus on the economy rather than on the social policies of previous Democratic candidates, Bill Clinton's election campaign came up with the slogan 'It's the economy, stupid.' Their rationale encapsulated neoliberal doctrine: whatever you might feel about social issues, people vote with their wallets and therefore economic policy must take priority.

This thinking underpinned both the failed presidential campaign of Hillary Clinton in 2016 and Britain's referendum on membership of the European Union. In both cases, centrists were shocked to discover that, for a majority of people, the smooth running of an economy that has excluded them and rewarded others is not their highest priority.

Of the key tenets of neoliberal ideology, by far the most pernicious is 'TINA'. It was Margaret Thatcher who popularised this term, sternly telling critics of her economic reforms that There Is No Alternative to globalised free market capitalism. It is this intransigent attitude that has driven voters to support populism.

Although it took root in the early 1980s, TINA gained even greater credence following the end of the Cold War. The swift demise of the Eastern Bloc, collapsing in the face of people power, was a happy ending that no one had predicted, so it is perhaps unsurprising that a fairy tale was woven by triumphant neoliberals to explain how we would all live happily ever after.

History, it was claimed, had come to an end. Communism had withered due to its internal contradictions, leaving the West victorious in the battle of ideas. Free markets, not tanks and troops, had liberated the subject peoples of Eastern Europe from totalitarian rule. Surely this was proof that Western liberal democracy was the final phase of human development?

However, in the decade that followed the fall of the Berlin Wall, oligarchs, corporations and other carpetbaggers were too busy bringing neoliberalism to the former Eastern Bloc to notice the rise of another economic system, one that was neither Western nor liberal and definitely not democratic. Twenty years after the fall of the Berlin Wall, China became the second-largest economy in the world and now has greater purchasing power than any other country.

Since 1945, the US and its European allies have promoted liberal democracy and free markets hand in hand as the best method for creating growth among emerging economies. The stimulus for this was the existence of an alternative economic model promoted by the Soviet Union. No matter how badly Western economies performed, they maintained the upper hand in this struggle, due to the fact that the Soviet economy was unable to successfully compete with the West. In China, however, the West has encountered an alternative economic model capable of beating neoliberal capitalism at its own game.

While maintaining a veneer of Maoist ideology, the Chinese Communist Party has developed a command economy geared towards consumerism. In the late 1980s, its stated aim was to make China a semi-industrialised country by the centenary of the People's Republic of China in 2049. Now it claims China will be a fully developed nation by that date, and all the evidence points towards the realisation of that goal. China already outstrips the world in terms of manufacturing and exports and is expected to overtake the US to become the world's largest economy in the next decade.

Observers estimate that, by 2020, there will be over 400 million consumers in China with a household income of between $16,000 and $32,000, a middle class larger than the entire population of the US. This economic success has been achieved under a one-party system which keeps tight control over freedom of expression, assembly, association and religion. In 2018, President Xi Jinping, the general secretary of the Communist Party of China, scrapped presidential term limits, making himself president for life.

In the past, the West used the promise of trade to encourage emerging economies to introduce democratic reforms: we will give you access to our goods and markets in return for the introduction of free and fair multi-party elections. Now Xi Jinping can offer a different model, one that does not require the implementation of pluralist democracy in order to trade with the world's most successful economy.

For despots around the world, the temptation to make deals with a major trading partner who doesn't demand that you recognise basic human rights is undoubtedly attractive. Some unstable nations may be tempted to turn their back on democracy and deal with their economic difficulties by following China's example of rapid economic growth through authoritarian rule.

Under the so-called Belt and Road Initiative, Chinese engineers are building infrastructure projects across Asia and Africa, replacing investment where Western power is waning. This massive project, coupled with Beijing's refusal to play by rules issuing from Western-controlled institutions, has shaken the world order created in the aftermath of World War II. Far from ending, history has shifted east in a sea change that challenges the long-held notion of Western hegemony.

Unsure of their position in the world as Western influence declines, voters in Europe and America have begun to turn inward, falling, as if in panic, upon the nation state as a means of taking back control from the forces of globalisation. Yet the neoliberals have little interest in national sovereignty. While they make a great show of raging against supranational bodies that seek to regulate the economy, their true commitment is to trade.

They may beat their chests patriotically as they speak of the people's sacred right to make their own laws, but the globalised economy has no respect for national borders. Neoliberals have ceded power to the bond markets. Their nation is an offshore tax haven and TINA is their creed.

Unable to respond to demands for change – TINA won't allow it – the neoliberal establishment has recently found its certainties challenged. Since the market crash of 2008, an ideological refusal to countenance any alternative to free market capitalism has driven voters into the arms of a new breed of populists, leaving the perplexed neoliberals on the sidelines waiting impatiently for the public to see sense and come back to the fiscal priorities that dictated policy around the turn of the twenty-first century.

Yet the pitch of the populist – a click-and-collect form of partisan democracy that promises to make everything great again – will only effect cosmetic changes to the neoliberal system. Like a placebo that fools the brain into releasing a jolt of pleasing endorphins, populism has little to offer the left-behind other than the visceral thrill of payback.

In order to correct the imbalance of power that produces low unemployment figures yet leaves record numbers of workers stranded below the poverty line, citizens must be given the opportunity to vote for policies that hold the markets to account.

2. EQUALITY

I disapprove of what you say, but I will defend to the death your right to say it.

The quote on the preceding page, widely attributed to Voltaire, was never uttered by the French philosopher. It was coined in the early twentieth century by a biographer as her interpretation of his viewpoint. Nevertheless, this expression of Voltaire's thinking resonates with such power that it has become the default example of the principle of free speech.

Although the words themselves are a summation, they confer on Voltaire the understanding that free speech alone is not enough to guarantee freedom. In order to be truly free, we have to respect the equal right of others to exercise the liberty that we claim for ourselves.

In offering to put his life on the line for the right of his opponent to express their view, Voltaire is taking a stand on equality. He is challenging our notion of freedom as an inalienable right that we take for granted, turning it instead into a question of character: are you willing to give a fair hearing to those you may disagree with?

In order to ensure that all voices are heard, equality – the responsibility to reciprocate the liberties that we enjoy – must be present to provide a second dimension to freedom. Working together, the one expanding the reach of the other, liberty and equality create an atmosphere of mutual respect in which we can each aspire to the 'Voltairian Principle'.

The vital link between freedom of speech and equality goes back to the very roots of democracy. The ancient Greeks developed a concept called *isegoria*, the equal right of all citizens to participate in public debate in the democratic assembly. Dating from around 2,500 years ago, *isegoria* was a defining aspect of Athenian democracy, allowing citizens from all strata of society to speak their mind in the public space.

It existed alongside another ancient concept of free speech practised by the citizens of Athens called *parrhesia*, the right to say whatever one wanted, whenever one wanted and to whomever one pleased. Neither of these rights was absolute.

Getting up to speak in the assembly could make you a target for the Athenian mob, while speaking your mind was sometimes fatal; Socrates lost his life because he told people what they didn't want to hear.

Today, the isegorian tradition of collective rights finds an echo in many legal definitions of freedom of expression. Under Article 10 of the European Convention on Human Rights, for example, an individual's right to freedom of expression must be balanced against the rights of society as a whole.

By contrast, *parrhesia* is reflected in the permissive definition of freedom of expression enshrined in the US constitution. Hate speech is largely protected, leading some commentators to fetishise the right to offend in the same manner that gun owners in the US feel the need to express their individual freedom by owning the largest and most rapid-firing automatic weapons.

America's commitment to free speech is such that, in 2010, the Supreme Court ruled corporations have the same rights of expression as individuals under the First Amendment. This decision made it impossible for citizens to limit the use of corporate funds to influence state and federal elections.

In recent American history, freedom of speech has been challenged by questions of who has the right to express an opinion. During the 1960s, civil rights, feminism and the Stonewall riots were all part of a push for greater equality, as marginalised communities struggled for the right to be heard. When the 1970s saw many progressive ideas enter the mainstream, America experienced a backlash with the election of Ronald Reagan in 1980. Encouraged by this rejection of liberal attitudes, conservative commentators began looking for socially acceptable ways to push back against the gains made by women, people of colour and the LGBT community. By the end of the 1980s, they were using the term 'political correctness' as a means to dismiss inclusive language and initiatives they felt uncomfortable with.

Quickly gaining currency among right-wing circles, the term allowed reactionaries to actively police the limits of social change, while at the same time implying that they themselves were the victims of some kind of conspiracy. Accusations of political correctness became part of the armoury deployed against those who challenged the status quo.

Universities have often been the front line in generational conflict, so it comes as no surprise that US campuses were already being excoriated for political correctness in the late 1980s. University of Chicago professor Allan Bloom wrote a book claiming that colleges were abandoning the canon of Western philosophy in favour of a multicultural approach. He had previously taught at Cornell and described his concern when, in 1969, African American students demanded the formation of a department to study the work of writers from their own culture, such as James Baldwin and Maya Angelou.

Bloom's book, *The Closing of the American Mind: How Higher Education Has Failed Democracy and Impoverished the Souls of Today's Students*, became a bestseller and sparked a series of investigations into an apparent trend towards what a

1990 *New York Times* article identified as 'a growing intolerance, a closing of debate, a pressure to conform'. The piece, 'The Rising Hegemony of the Politically Correct' by Richard Bernstein, helped introduce the term to public consciousness.

'Instead of writing about literary classics and other topics, as they have in the past,' he began, 'freshmen at the University of Texas next fall will base their compositions on a packet of essays on discrimination, affirmative-action and civil-rights cases. The new program, called "Writing on Difference", was voted in by the faculty last month and has been praised by many professors for giving the curriculum more relevance to real-life concerns. But some see it as a stifling example of academic orthodoxy.'

Bernstein quoted Roger Kimball, author of *Tenured Radicals: How Politics Has Corrupted Our Higher Education*, who described political correctness as a form of 'liberal fascism'. 'Under the name of pluralism and freedom of speech,' Kimball stated, '[political correctness] is an attempt to enforce a narrow and ideologically motivated view of both the curriculum and what it means to be an educated person, a responsible citizen.'

Far from narrowing the curriculum, students were seeking to broaden the scope of their education by including other voices. However, their critics made little attempt to investigate why they might have wished to do so.

In 1963, when Cornell became the first Ivy League college to instigate a programme to increase the enrolment and support of African American students, Allan Bloom was already on the faculty. He must have known that the demand for an African American studies centre arose in response to the appearance of a burning cross outside the black women's cooperative on campus. Yet this was never mentioned in his book.

In their determination to defend the Western canon, Bloom, Bernstein and Kimball were unable to see that they were guilty of the very sins they ascribed to the radical students: a growing intolerance; a determination to close down debate; the need to pressure others into conformity; the imposition of an orthodoxy.

In the debate over political correctness, the Voltairian Principle of equal respect for those you disagree with appears to have been discarded by those claiming to defend freedom of speech. What was it about the idea of inclusivity that drove them to such measures?

Every nation relies on an educated elite from which to draw its administrators. In most countries, these are the product of a small number of exclusive colleges that provide an education based on the Western classical tradition. It furnishes graduates with a common frame of reference and a sense of entitlement that opens doors to the corridors of power.

Bloom (Chicago), Bernstein (Harvard) and Kimball (Yale) are all products of such a system. If the orthodoxy they followed were to be challenged, perhaps superseded, by other criteria that they were not party to, how could they maintain their status within society? Exclusivity was the key to their power and thus it had to be defended against the inclusive intentions of outsiders.

This battle still rages in academia today. Niall Ferguson (Oxford) rails against 'grievance studies'; Jordan Peterson (McGill) sees 'cultural Marxism' at work everywhere. This negative labelling represents a determined attempt to control the agenda, to decide who is entitled to speak and who is not, and, ultimately, to define the meaning of liberty itself.

In 2018, Eric Weinstein, an American investment banker, coined the term 'Intellectual Dark Web' to describe a loose grouping of contrarians who believe that they are being excluded from mainstream media due to their refusal to bow to political correctness.

Given that these freedom fighters include Jordan Peterson (whose tour in support of his best-selling book sold out venues associated with rock stars), Joe Rogan (host of three-hour-long YouTube discussions that can garner over a million views) and Ben Shapiro (a podcaster who attracts 15 million listeners a month) among their number, it's hard to see how they can claim to be marginalised. Yet they revel in the status of pariahs.

Although they have no official ideology, members of the grouping see themselves as staunch defenders of free speech. In a long and widely reported 'coming out' article in the *New York Times*, journalist Bari Weiss summed up the ethos of the Intellectual Dark Web as being 'committed to the belief that setting up no-go zones and no-go people is inherently corrupting to free thought'. Yet their willingness to extend that right to their opponents is sadly lacking.

Weinstein, who since naming the group has emerged as a leading spokesman, recorded an interview, posted in early 2019, on the Rebel Wisdom website entitled 'Inside the Intellectual Dark Web'. His commitment to free speech seemed to have little in common with that attributed to Voltaire.

'It's very important to me,' he told interviewer David Fuller, 'that not only do we not spend time debating people who are not serious in their intellectualism, but that we realise that it is important to the diversity of mature and important ideas that we not spend undue effort engaging ideas that are functioning very differently from regular conversation.'

Just as the original promoters of the political correctness myth resorted to the very tactics that they were loudly criticising, so the denizens of the Intellectual Dark Web seem eager to set up their own no-go zones and no-go people. This reactionary tendency is not uncommon among the loudest proponents of free speech.

On 2 July 2018, former Republican senator and Libertarian Party candidate Ron Paul tweeted, 'Are you stunned by what has become of American culture? Well, it's not an accident. You've probably heard of "Cultural Marxism", but do you know what it means?' Attached to the tweet was a crude cartoon of Uncle Sam being knocked out by a giant red fist with a hammer and sickle adorning its arm. The punch was being delivered by four racist stereotypes: a bearded, hook-nosed Jew; a yellow-faced, buck-toothed Oriental; a boss-eyed Latino; and a grinning African. Together they shout, 'Cultural Marxism!'

Following complaints, the tweet was quickly removed and Paul apologised for the offence caused. Yet many wondered how a self-declared libertarian could mount such an illiberal argument. Brian Doherty, writing on the libertarian website Reason, drew attention to a statement that Paul had made on his online TV series, itself on the subject of 'cultural Marxism': 'Liberty means allowing [everybody] to make personal choices, personal social relationship, personal sexual choices, personal economic choices.' That, he said, should not be a 'threat'; it should 'bring people together'.

The difference between Paul's measured statement before the cameras on his TV series and the bigotry evidenced by his use of the offensive meme highlights the manner in which social media has debased the currency of online discourse. Paul had clearly given some thought to the condemnation of cultural Marxism he broadcast on TV, reaching into his own libertarian principles to recognise the rights of others to freely make their own decisions, even though they may be opposed to his own.

Yet Paul's online persona recognised no such distinction; the immediacy of social media betrayed his principles to such an extent that he was forced to delete the image and apologise. This irrational urge to post outrageous statements with scant prior consideration is a hallmark of online debate, an indication that social media has punctured the division between private and public freedom.

In the privacy of your own home, you may stretch out in a favourite armchair, kicking your shoes off and making ample use of the armrests. Yet if you try to relax in the same manner next to a stranger in an economy-class seat on a packed airliner, you're very likely to find your behaviour challenged. Legs akimbo, elbows out, you're invading the personal space of another individual which needs to be respected if you're intending to fly economy.

You may see someone in another seat spreading themselves, fast asleep on the shoulder of the passenger next to them, but you can be sure that those two are either related in some way or very good friends, and so have a respect for one another that allows behaviour that would otherwise be transgressive. If you are not willing to respect everyone equally, then your liberty to do as you wish in a public place will likely be met with admonishment.

Context is key. At home in your comfort zone, you are free to act and speak as you wish. In public, different rules apply. You are still free to act and express your opinion, but you are conscious of the demeanour of those around you. Years of people-watching have made us adept at judging the mood of the strangers we encounter.

The way that you deport yourself will have been shaped by your visual assessment of the person before you. Gender, age, ethnicity – all will be factored into how you interact, if indeed you do. A person may not want interaction, and you must be alert to that signal too. Whatever reaction you get, mutual respect is the key to getting through the day without confrontation.

But what if you're in a public place and you can't see the stranger you've encountered? Social media takes the private freedom derived from being in your own space and places it in a public forum. Without clear visual signals to moderate your interaction, the lines between reaction and responsibility become blurred.

For some social media users, this offers opportunities to act in ways they would never dare contemplate in real-world, face-to-face interactions. Online anonymity can create an atmosphere where bullying, pile-ons and abusive language are never far from the surface. Although it may feel like a cloak of invisibility, anonymity turns liberty into licence by removing both behavioural limits and consequences.

This explains why, among the more belligerent online communities, there can be no greater crime than doxing, the sharing of information that identifies an individual, opening them up to the consequences of their behaviour in the real, offline world.

The potential for online behaviour to spill over into our everyday lives has been a driver of the trend towards the creation of safe spaces at our universities. Digital natives are well aware that expressions of support for inclusivity will often attract trolls addicted to offending the sensibilities of those they dismiss as 'social justice warriors'. While such behaviour can be blocked online, dealing with disruptive forces in the real world poses a greater challenge.

While much of the controversy around safe spaces has focused on how they might be used to prevent opinions being heard, their actual purpose is to ensure that everyone has the opportunity to express their opinion free from harassment and discrimination. Safe-space rules drawn up by student bodies in the UK make it clear that the aim of this policy is to create an environment in which all students, staff and visitors feel welcome, respected and able to fully participate in events and activities.

Safe spaces are deemed necessary because students are aware that certain social structures may serve to disadvantage particular groups. In seeking to address this problem, safe-space policy often calls for zero tolerance of harassment, abuse, discrimination and violence on campus. In this sense, it is similar in scope to the legislation that governs behaviour in the workplace.

The aim of these guidelines is to establish mutual consent among speakers about the tone of any given debate. Rather than seeking to control what can and cannot be discussed, safe-space policy sets out to moderate the ambience of the debate, to ensure that all opinions are considered in an atmosphere of inclusivity. It is designed to bring the dimensions of equality and accountability into harmony with the liberty afforded by free speech.

The need for safe spaces has arisen because, historically, the far right has often used provocation as a tactic against those it seeks to marginalise. Think of Oswald Mosley trying to march his British Union of Fascists through the Jewish neighbourhoods of London's East End in the 1930s, or the neo-Nazi National Front holding their meetings in Southall, the centre of London's Asian community, during the late 1970s.

The desocialising nature of online discourse has allowed a new generation of would-be demagogues to find a following through social media. Under the guise of free speech campaigns, they have taken their angry rhetoric onto the streets, seeking to provoke confrontation.

Portland, Oregon has recently become a magnet for far-right provocateurs in the US. A city known for its progressive culture, Portland has become a target for demonstrations by a group called Patriot Prayer, who claim to be defending the right to free speech. Despite their name, they appear to have no religious overtones nor any specific ideology. Their leader, Joey Gibson, has admitted that the idea that brings them together is nothing more than 'hatred of the Left'. As such, they represent an angry online forum made flesh, driven by little more than an urge to offend.

In June 2018, truthout.org, an independent non-profit news organisation covering social justice issues, carried a report of a Patriot Prayer demonstration in Portland. 'Without a statement of purpose or any planned speeches, Gibson's supporters . . . showed up ready to fight from the moment they entered the park. Their anger was pointed directly at the several hundred anti-fascist protesters quartered across the street at another length of the park . . . No politics were on the agenda that day, no talk of the issues Gibson had set his "campaign" on, nor what he insisted Patriot Prayer stood for. Instead, the event was centered entirely on a street brawl with the "left".'

This is the politics of presence: if your goal is nothing more than the domination of the public square, then violent disruption is as good a weapon as argument; better, perhaps, for it dispenses with the need for civility. Anyone who is familiar with the way anger can quickly boil over into abuse during an online debate will recognise this tactic. It presents a genuine challenge to those who believe in freedom of speech.

How best to deal with the belligerent speaker who demands impunity for their views and a space in which to voice them? Freedom of speech does not guarantee you a platform from which to air your opinions. You may hold trenchant views on a number of subjects but the fact that *The*

Times won't print your ruminations doesn't mean you are being oppressed.

The tactic of no-platforming favoured by some social justice activists can be counterproductive, giving a provocative speaker the opportunity to portray themselves as a martyr to their followers. The task of revealing the true intent of those who mask their prejudices in rhetoric and performance requires that we give them space to air their offensive views.

However, white, middle-aged men and women in the privileged position of not being the target of daily discrimination and abuse should not presume to tell the victims of such treatment that they must subject themselves to being lectured by their tormentors. There are situations where it is necessary to ask whether providing a platform may only serve to empower the forces of prejudice.

If only for the fact that so much great culture has been made by those willing to break taboos, freedom of expression must uphold the right to offend, shock or disturb. However, it is a liberty that should be exercised with care: when vindictive, offence can easily mutate into abuse. Where that point occurs is a matter for debate. Because offence is subjective, each of us has our own sense of its limits, although the argument that offence ends and abuse begins where things get personal would appear to have broad support on social media.

'If liberty means anything at all,' wrote George Orwell in an essay intended as the preface to *Animal Farm*, 'it means the right to tell people what they do not want to hear.' Penned in 1943, the essay offers a good definition of the freedom to dissent that is the fundamental principle of free speech. The patron saint of the dissenting tradition, Orwell's defence of liberty was not, however, intended at some time in the future to provide justification to an angry mob of keyboard warriors determined to tell a woman that she deserved to be raped and killed because she spoke in defence of inclusivity in video games.

'If the intellectual liberty which without a doubt has been one of the distinguishing marks of western civilisation means anything at all,' he wrote in the same essay, 'it means that everyone shall have the right to say and to print what he believes to be the truth, provided only that it does not harm the rest of the community in some quite unmistakable way.'

When Orwell uses the word 'provided' in that sentence, he's articulating the dividing line between dissent and abuse. While freedom of speech gives you the right to dissent and, yes, to offend, it does not give you the right to abuse. You may be very concerned about gender issues within video games, but if you're unable to articulate those concerns without being abusive, then you must expect to be held to account for your behaviour.

Orwell's 'provided' also illuminates the crucial difference between the manner in which the Intellectual Dark Web and the safe-space movement approach the issue of freedom of speech. Eric Weinstein makes clear in his comments to Rebel Wisdom that dissent is not to be tolerated at the high table that he and his colleagues have created. By contrast, the rules of the safe-space movement accommodate dissent, but are designed to ensure that there is no tolerance for abusive speech or behaviour.

In his refusal to recognise the reciprocal nature of freedom – that you must respect in others the rights that you claim for yourself – Weinstein reveals the Intellectual Dark Web to be party to the strain of irate exceptionalism that runs through the new generation of free speech warriors.

Obsessed with hierarchy and their position in it, they will brook no questioning of their privilege and prejudices. For them, freedom is a one-dimensional construct that stands or falls on their right to express an opinion. Demanding to be heard, yet refusing to listen, it's not free speech that they want, it's free rein – to say whatever they wish without challenge or consequence.

To counter the pernicious idea that freedom means being free from restraint requires that we confer on equality and accountability the same high regard we currently give to free speech. In this manner, we can maintain the balance necessary for all voices to be heard and respected, and thus restore the inclusivity that true freedom demands.

3. ACCOUNTABILITY

What's happened to that twat David
Cameron who called it on? How comes
he can scuttle off? . . . Where is the
geezer? I think he should be held to
account for it.

—Danny Dyer

When he quipped that the nine most terrifying words in the English language are 'I'm from the government and I'm here to help', Ronald Reagan was endorsing Friedrich Hayek's one-dimensional notion of liberty as freedom from restraint. While it is true that the rules and regulations that governments introduce do create more bureaucracy, their aim is to ensure that business is conducted in an environment that is both safe for employees and customers and transparent in its practices.

In the unequal struggle between the rights of the citizen and those of corporations, the paperwork follows the power. Red tape is agency made flesh, which is why it is so often the target of neoliberal ire. From Reagan onwards, successive American presidents have dismantled legislation enacted by Franklin Roosevelt that aimed to bring greater transparency to the financial sector following the Wall Street Crash.

Roosevelt's tight fiscal policies created the stability that led to post-war prosperity, yet by the 1990s, corporate capture of the democratic process had seen them steadily watered down. Financial transactions became opaque just as trading moved online, making it even more difficult for anyone – regulators, bankers or investors – to know what was really going on beneath the surface. As a result of deregulation, banks took on greater risks until, in 2008, the neoliberal reliance on cheap credit rather than higher wages to stimulate growth came home to roost.

The realisation that many low-income homeowners in the US were never going to repay their mortgages created a crisis in the global banking system. The ensuing chaos was so great that the Queen was moved to ask a gathering of academics at the London School of Economics why none of them had seen the crash coming. They shrugged and told her that, at every stage, someone was relying on somebody else and everyone thought they were doing the right thing. Or, to put it another way: 'I'm from the free market and I'm not here to help.'

The 2008 crash was a crisis of accountability, not capitalism. The problems caused by the free market are systemic in nature, the result of choices that have been made. Given the right tools, we can work together to make better choices, ones that benefit the whole of society and not just those whose lofty position in the power structure is based on their immense wealth. In terms of its relationship to human agency, capitalism is like fire: keep it under control and it will give you heat and light; leave it untended and it will consume everything in its path.

Throughout history, crises of accountability have been the catalysts for advances in individual agency. The Magna Carta, drawn up in thirteenth-century England as a counter to the absolute power of the monarchy, evolved over several decades into a bill of rights that went on to shape law on both sides of the Atlantic. The decision of Henry VIII to break with Rome in the 1530s was a response to the unaccountable power of the papacy, and it led to a flowering of religious dissent in England.

In the seventeenth century, the insistence of

Charles I on the Divine Right of Kings to rule without consulting parliament led to civil war. The conflict raged across England, Scotland, Ireland and Wales, only ending with an act of accountability *in extremis*: the beheading of a king. While it was not uncommon for monarchs to be killed in combat, murdered in secret or dispatched by summary execution, in 1649, for the first time in English history, a monarch was put to death in accordance with the law.

In their determination to hold Charles to account – and to be accountable themselves – parliament put the king on trial for treason. This was an unprecedented step. Previously, treason had been defined as an act against the crown. In a direct challenge to the absolute power of the executive, parliament redefined treason as an act against the state.

The execution of Charles I had been forced upon the parliamentarians. They had not taken up arms against the king to depose him but rather to assert their right to rule by consent. His intransigence, even in captivity, was the reason for his trial and execution, and the result was a de facto republic that no one had planned for. From the start there were problems, not least because the republic was embodied in the power of one man, Oliver Cromwell, whose abuse of parliament was almost as bad as that of Charles before him.

Yet the lack of a republican tradition in England was also a factor. A century and a half would pass before Thomas Paine published *The Rights of Man*. Had Cromwell's New Model Army been carrying that incendiary pamphlet in their knapsacks at Naseby, the English republic may well have flourished.

Instead, it barely outlived Cromwell. The monarchy was restored in 1660, but the idea that had inspired the Roundheads to take up arms was not forgotten. When they later raised toasts to what they called the 'Good Old Cause', it was the struggle to hold absolute power to account that they were keeping faith with, not republicanism. That faith was called into action again in 1688, when the behaviour of another English king led once again to a crisis of accountability.

Like his father, James II wanted to be an absolute monarch. Modelling his reign on that of his contemporary, Louis XIV of France, the all-powerful 'Sun King', he sought to rule by decree. James's absolutism and his promotion of the Catholic nobility led to his downfall in 1688, when parliament invited William of Orange, a Dutch Protestant who was married to James's daughter Mary, to invade England and depose the king.

After a few skirmishes, James fled. Many members of parliament had been young men during the civil war and had witnessed that time of chaos and carnage at first hand. By contrast, the bloodshed that accompanied the parliamentary *coup d'état* of 1688 was minor, leading contemporary historians to christen it the 'Glorious Revolution'.

Before William and Mary took the throne, they were required to sign a bill of rights protecting parliament from absolutism. This guaranteed regular parliaments, free and fair elections and freedom of speech in parliament. The 1689 Bill of Rights was the first document of its kind to be ratified by a monarch, creating a framework of accountability around the use of executive power. It influenced the US Constitution and the French Declaration of the Rights of Man.

However, unlike those later documents guaranteeing the liberties of citizens, the English Bill of Rights was an agreement between the crown and parliament. Some rights were granted to all Englishmen, but most of the provisions applied only to members of parliament. Despite its limitations, the Bill of Rights was the realisation of the 'Good Old Cause', providing the basis for rule by consent.

While the constitutional monarchy created by the settlement of 1689 laid the foundations of the modern British state, it was the last time that parliament sought to codify the relationship between the rulers and the ruled.

The British constitution is said to be 'unwritten', in the sense that the fundamental rights of the individual are not gathered together in a single charter to which all citizens can refer. There

is no document that begins 'We, the People . . .'
Instead, individual rights are contained in laws, practices and legal conventions, some of which date back to the Magna Carta.

The strength of this uncodified arrangement is that the constitution can easily be updated if circumstances necessitate it. Unfortunately, that is also its weakness. A constitution is a set of rules by which citizens consent to be governed. If those rules can be changed by a simple majority vote in parliament, then the immutable nature of individual rights is compromised.

In 1950, the Council of Europe, an intergovernmental organisation founded to uphold human rights, the rule of law and democracy in the wake of World War II, produced the European Convention on Human Rights (ECHR), which was ratified by all of the member states, including the UK.

Following a 1966 act of parliament with which the UK government granted them the ability to take court cases to the European Court of Human Rights in Strasbourg, British citizens were able to access the rights enshrined in the ECHR. However, rights are meaningless if you cannot enforce them, and the expense of taking a case all the way to the European Court was prohibitive.

In 1998, the ECHR was incorporated into UK law by the Labour government of Tony Blair, making a remedy for breach of the convention available in British courts. While believing that they should be inalienable and available to all citizens, Blair viewed the granting of rights as a transactional exchange. Where Thatcher had declared that there was no such thing as society and post-war Labour had provided welfare for all, he sought a third way.

Writing in the *Guardian* in 2002, the then prime minister explained his thinking: 'As the 1980s had progressed I sensed increasingly that the task for the centre-Left was not to replace crude individualism with an overbearing paternalistic state. It was to rebuild a strong civic society where rights and duties go hand in hand.'

Blair understood that rights grant the power of

accountability to the individual. In return for that concession, he sought to place a duty upon the citizen to moderate their behaviour. By making such a demand, he inadvertently drew attention to the crucial difference between responsibility and accountability.

When we talk of 'taking responsibility', the use of the transitive verb 'to take' reveals responsibility to be the possession of the individual. Conversely, when we speak of 'holding to account', the implication of being held is that an external force acts upon us. It's a small but important distinction. Responsibility requires that we maintain authority over our own behaviour; accountability gives us a degree of authority over the behaviour of others.

This explains why the incorporation of the ECHR was not welcomed by all sections of society. This significant enhancement of individual agency challenged the convention of Britain's uncodified constitution. By gathering citizens' fundamental rights together in a single document, it seriously narrowed the wriggle room that the British establishment had exploited for centuries.

Opposition to the ECHR took the form of outrage at what was perceived to be the licence for political correctness inherent in its application. During the 2005 general election, Conservative Party leader Michael Howard promised to remove the convention from British law. He was reported to have warned that the politically correct regime ushered in by Labour's enthusiastic adoption of human rights legislation had turned the age-old principle of fairness on its head.

At the Conservative Party Conference in October 2011, the then home secretary, Theresa May, made a speech attacking the act that had incorporated the ECHR into British law. 'We all know the stories about the Human Rights Act,' she told the party faithful, '. . . about the illegal immigrant who cannot be deported because, and I am not making this up, he had a pet cat.'

In fact, she *was* making it up. The man in question could not be removed because May's department had failed to follow its own rules allowing partners of UK citizens leave to remain if they could prove they had been together for over two years. The immigrant had been living with his girlfriend for four years so was eligible to stay in the UK, cat or no cat.

Such spurious accusations of political correctness have also been a key component of Tory opposition to the European Union. The mischievous mendacity of Boris Johnson's anti-Brussels broadsides in the *Daily Telegraph* may seem frivolous, with their complaints about EU legislation to ban bent bananas and prawn-cocktail-flavoured crisps, but they mask a serious agenda.

After forty years of neoliberalism, the UK is the second-least-regulated market among the thirty-six nations of the Organisation for Economic Co-operation and Development (OECD), an intergovernmental forum aimed at seeking solutions to common economic and social problems. Britain's workers have far fewer rights than those in other EU countries.

Legislation from the EU challenges the British mania for deregulation. Recent moves by Brussels to bring transparency to the financial sector have been fiercely resisted by the City of London. Right-wing British papers may have defended the curvature of bananas to make the case for Brexit, but their real agenda was the avoidance of EU legislative accountability.

The EU's Working Time Directive (which limits the working week to forty-eight hours), the Temporary Agency Work Directive (giving equal rights to agency employees) and the Anti-Tax Avoidance Directive (which does what it says on the tin) all threatened to reverse years of neoliberal deregulation and light-touch taxation which successive British governments have championed.

The slogan of the official Vote Leave campaign in the 2016 referendum on Britain's EU membership made reference to the desire to avoid having to implement these directives. 'Let's Take Back Control' is seen as a masterful encapsulation of the British demand for a return of national sovereignty. This repatriation is much heralded by those who stand by their decision to vote for Brexit.

Yet, in this instance, taking back control does not confer greater agency on citizens. The return of sovereignty to the UK parliament means that there will be no higher authority scrutinising its behaviour than the British constitution, which parliament itself commands. For the Tory deregulationists who were driving the Leave campaign, the 'Let's Take Back Control' slogan had a subordinate clause: '. . . to Avoid Being Held to Account.'

The fact that the UK was unable to get its own way was seen as a key motivating issue for the campaign to leave the EU. The official Vote Leave website complained bitterly about the democratic deficit in Brussels, although only in so much as the UK didn't have enough power.

'The UK has so few votes that *we can't block EU laws.* We can only rely on having 8 per cent of votes in the Council of Ministers and have less than 10 per cent of the votes in the European Parliament. Politicians have *surrendered the UK's power to veto laws we disagree with*, so if the EU decides to introduce a law that will be bad for Britain there is nothing we can do to stop it.'

Unlike the British tradition of a malleable constitution conferring power on the party that has a majority in the Commons, the diverse nature of an institution representing twenty-eight nations means that there is no single party or ideology in control of the EU. Majorities have to be constructed over every issue. In such an atmosphere, it's understandable that British exceptionalism would fail to win every debate.

With their permanent seat on the UN Security Council and their primary role in NATO, the British are used to getting their way. You can hear it in the shock expressed on the Leave campaign website. Their demand for a veto on EU laws and parliamentary representation out of all proportion to Britain's size betrays a sense of entitlement that fails to recognise the UK's place in the world today.

The sad fact is that when Conservative ministers have to sit around the table and be coaxed into making some accommodation with the other twenty-seven members, they can't help but feel that they are part of someone else's empire.

The EU is not without its faults. The process of finding a consensus can be slow and frustrating, so there is a tendency to look to technocratic solutions. Where member states have proved unwilling to conform to rules on fiscal rectitude, the EU has sent in unelected technocrats to cut wages, slash spending and privatise the public sector.

Clearly, the EU is a work in progress and reform is needed to ensure it is more accountable to its citizens. Yet in an age when the great issues of the day – climate change, tax avoidance, the power of algorithms – challenge us on a global level, the ability of the nation state to respond is limited. Competition has divided society; healing it requires cooperation and, albeit unsteady at times, the EU is forging a path in that direction.

Brexit is part of a recent trend that has seen nations turn their backs on the multinational institutions that have sought to create collective solutions to global problems. Where the US once took a leading role in encouraging this process, the election of Donald Trump on an 'America First' platform has led to a more transactional approach to diplomacy. 'Moving forward,' he told the UN in September 2018, 'we are only going to give foreign aid to those who respect us and, frankly, are our friends.' His doctrine of acquiescence before aid is reflected in other attempts to unpick treaties that fail to recognise American authority.

Trump used the same speech to reject the idea that America could be held accountable for its actions, refusing to recognise the International Criminal Court. 'We reject the ideology of globalism,' he said, referring not to the neoliberal project but to the institutions that seek to police it, 'and we embrace the doctrine of patriotism.'

When Samuel Johnson observed that patriotism is the last refuge of the scoundrel, he was commenting on scoundrels, not patriotism. None of us can choose the family into which we are born; likewise the community, culture and country of our birth. Though we may reject all when first finding our way in the world, a sense of belonging is a powerful emotion. A blessing and a curse, it can be a source of pride and disappointment in equal measure.

In the hands of scoundrels, that sense of belonging can be exploited for divisive ends. When Trump seeks to turn love for one's country into a political doctrine, he's using patriotism as a shield. 'My country, right or wrong' brooks no criticism, never mind accountability.

But then Trump never has been troubled by responsibility. His shocking statement that he 'could stand in the middle of Fifth Avenue and shoot somebody' and still not lose voters was couched in the characteristic hubris of a man who has been walking away from accountability his whole adult life. Trump's reliance on the willingness of his supporters to find some justification for him pulling the trigger wasn't merely a rejection of the notion of being held to account, it was a smug assertion that it wouldn't matter even if he were.

As a stark illustration of the demise of our ability to resolve issues through deliberation and democracy, it has echoes in the UK's Brexit debate. When, during the referendum, Michael Gove declared that people in Britain had had enough of experts, he was turning his back on the notion of an enlightened electorate making informed decisions via the ballot box. Instead, the most complex issue in British post-war history was decided with scant regard to facts.

This situation is not helped by a media that amplifies the differences of opinion that are the lifeblood of a democratic society. Disputes drive clicks, so every interviewer tries to sniff out that 'gotcha' moment that will light up social media. In this charged atmosphere, policies come a poor second to personalities.

Cartoonish, confrontational characters are encouraged, given licence to sound off and, if they produce ratings, taken seriously by the mainstream. Politicians in this mould are lauded for their straight-talking style, a quality that often betrays an inability to consult, delegate or grasp nuance.

This is a time of dismissive demagogues promoting a know-nothing politics of swaggering arrogance driven by scorn and spite. Our ability to have a respectful disagreement with our opponents has been torn to shreds by market forces in a deliberate act of irresponsibility.

In 1949, the US Federal Communications Commission introduced a fairness doctrine that required broadcasters to cover controversial issues of public importance and to do so in a manner that presented both sides of the argument. The aim of the FCC was to ensure that a diversity of opinions was heard, no matter which medium or channel the public tuned in to.

Shortly after he became president, Ronald Reagan appointed a new chairman to the FCC, Mark S. Fowler, who took office in 1981 determined to implement Reagan's deregulation agenda across the broadcasting industries. In August 1987, he succeeded in abolishing the fairness doctrine on the grounds that it infringed the First Amendment rights of journalists by denying their free speech in editorial decisions.

The First Amendment to the US Constitution guarantees freedom of religion, worship, speech, press, assembly and redress. It is implicitly pluralistic in intent, giving constitutional protection to a diversity of dissent. Yet the abolition of the fairness doctrine failed to uphold that ideal. Firstly, it sought to silence opposing voices; secondly, it opened up the market for partisan broadcasting.

By giving free speech primacy over accountability, Fowler made the rise of Fox News – or something very like it – an inevitability. A year after the abolition, on 1 August 1988, right-wing pundit Rush Limbaugh launched his nationally syndicated radio show. Highly popular with listeners, he proved that there was a market for conservative broadcasting. Within a decade, the format came to dominate commercial talk radio in the US and spawned similar programming on cable TV.

With its commitment to listen respectfully to diverse opinions, the fairness doctrine had been an expression of the Voltairian Principle. Its abolition created a safe space for conservatives to disseminate their views without challenge. In removing the dimension of equality from broadcasting, the Reagan administration made it more difficult to hold those in power to account and contributed to the polarisation of opinion that we see today.

If there is anything in need of a modern version of the fairness doctrine, it is undoubtedly social media. The digital domains that so many of us inhabit are ruled by consent, inasmuch as we have all agreed to the terms and conditions presented to us on signing up to our favourite sites. Yet there is more than an element of absolutism in the behaviour of the social media empires that offer us freedom of expression on a scale unimaginable a generation ago.

While we avidly broadcast details of our personal lives to the world, the liberty that we are enjoying is being monitored and the data collected. Algorithms designed to streamline our online experience also have us under surveillance. How do we hold them to account?

Most of us are aware of the transactional nature of social media. Our parents' warning that we should never take cookies from strangers has long been discarded as our curiosity takes us deeper into the entanglements of the World Wide

Web. While most of us don't mind websites making a living from our visits, evidence has emerged that the information we freely give up has been used for political gain.

In 2018, the US Senate Select Committee on Intelligence reported that Russian troll factories had mounted campaigns on social media sites with the aim of suppressing support for the Democratic Party during the 2016 election. Posting on Facebook, Twitter, Instagram, YouTube, Reddit, Tumblr, Pinterest, Vine and Google+, Russian operatives had created thousands of accounts under fake names and set about sowing distrust and fomenting polarisation among targeted groups.

In 2018, it was revealed that a British political consulting firm had mined the data of an estimated 87 million Facebook users without their knowledge. Cambridge Analytica had paid 32,000 US voters to take a personality test, which also contained political questions, via an app that required them to log in through their Facebook accounts.

The app surreptitiously collected data about their likes and those of all their Facebook friends. When the results of the personality test were compared with the information from their Facebook accounts, it was possible to discern psychological patterns.

Algorithms then extrapolated the findings of the original 32,000 participants into a data set that could predict the political outlook of millions of Facebook users. That is incredibly valuable data for political campaigns looking to micro-target people with information that could either enforce or undermine their political views. Evidence also emerged to suggest that Cambridge Analytica had been involved in the Brexit referendum, working with the campaign to leave the EU.

Facebook's power – it also owns Instagram and WhatsApp – is greatly enhanced by the dominance it enjoys in the social media market. Globalisation has allowed it and other digital monopolies like Google and Apple to develop an extractive business model that makes money from customers in many different jurisdictions, while declaring the bulk of their profits in the country with the lightest tax regime. As a result, regulators have difficulty in holding the company to account.

However, the Cambridge Analytica data breach has drawn attention to the potential hazards of allowing algorithms access to personal information, no matter how trivial. The more that artificial intelligence becomes involved in our everyday lives, the greater transparency we need about what it is doing and who is programming it.

While waiting for governments to regulate the tech giants, citizens have been utilising the internet to demand accountability. Following the acquittal of George Zimmerman for the shooting of unarmed teen Trayvon Martin in Florida in 2012, the hashtag #BlackLivesMatter began drawing global attention to the killings of African American men by police and vigilantes.

The Me Too movement, highlighting sexual harassment and sexual assault, was founded by Tarana Burke in 2006. In 2017, following allegations of sexual abuse against the film producer

Harvey Weinstein, #MeToo trended on Twitter as women around the world sought to highlight the magnitude of the problem by alluding to or describing their own experiences of abuse.

In February 2018, #NeverAgain began trending on Facebook following the murder of seventeen students and staff at the Marjory Stoneman Douglas High School in Parkland, Florida. A group of survivors began a campaign for legislative action to prevent similar shootings happening again. They gained over 35,000 followers in just three days and became an active focus for the gun control movement in the US.

The screens in our pockets have undoubtedly enhanced the ability of citizens to build solidarity in the struggle for genuine change. Taking our inspiration from accountability movements such as #BlackLivesMatter, #MeToo and #NeverAgain, we need to use the connectivity we enjoy to renew the reciprocal obligations that create the framework for a cohesive society.

The need for collective action is nowhere more urgent than in response to our changing climate.

It's hard to ignore the fact that the planet is getting warmer, in terms of both the scientific evidence and the extreme weather events we experience first-hand, yet denial of this phenomenon is still given currency by elected officials.

For neoliberals, the idea that climate change is man-made runs counter to their ideology. Economists for Free Trade, a British-based lobbying group pushing for deregulation which includes Jacob Rees-Mogg and Sir James Dyson among its advisors, maintains strong links to climate change denial. The EFT's convener, Edgar Miller, made his fortune by investing in the US shale gas industry and has been named as a founder and funder of a climate-science-denying organisation, the Global Warming Policy Foundation, which is chaired by former British chancellor Nigel Lawson.

Their fear is that, in order to mitigate the effects of climate change, environmental concerns will have to take precedence over market forces. To create sustainable economic growth will require corporations to be accountable for their practices, yet such is their aversion to regulatory democracy that neoliberals are willing to argue that, although the planet's climate is rapidly changing, its economic system cannot.

Yet the Divine Right of Kings once seemed an unalterable fact too. The challenge that faced the English in the seventeenth century was how to curb the absolute power of the monarch. In the twenty-first century, it is the markets that have taken on the mantle of absolutism, placing themselves above the jurisdiction of national governments. Holding the king to account was unprecedented and went against custom and tradition – holding the global markets to account is just as audacious and just as necessary.

For the moment, the populists have the upper hand in this battle, but their methods are divisive, seeking to split the nation into hostile camps: old vs young, men vs women, black vs white, somewhere vs nowhere.

When it comes to freedom, what people most desire is the security that comes from having a degree of agency over one's life. A 2018 poll of

English citizens found that only 21 per cent think they can influence their local decision-making process. For many of us, power is wielded far away by people who don't share our own lived experiences.

This is the alienating nature of neoliberal democracy: whereas in the past, social democracy generated local profit through local employment, the extractive capitalism encouraged by globalisation takes but does not provide. As a result, people are angry.

While some of the poorest in society voted for Trump in the US and Brexit in the UK, and wore the *gilet jaune* in France, the majority of the support for these movements comes from those who are doing okay but feel they should really be doing better. Unhappy with their lot, they find that the narrow options made available by neoliberal democracy leave them with little choice but to revolt. As recent events have shown, if they are not offered meaningful change, they are prepared to vote wilfully for damn-the-lot-of-you chaos.

Rather than relying on the whims of benign authoritarians or the largesse of multinational corporations, people deserve the security of health, employment and tenancy that comes from having some form of agency. Accountability is the key to creating a civic revolution.

A programme of democratic reform that decentralises power and makes everyone's vote count is desperately needed if we hope to re-engage citizens in deliberative democracy. Voting rights must be guaranteed for all and electoral districts drawn up by an independent commission. In order that elected office not be limited to millionaires, we need restrictions on campaign financing. Lobbyists and think tanks should be subject to strict transparency rules to ensure we know who is paying for the information we receive.

For many low-skilled workers, the casualisation of labour means that work no longer provides them with a route out of poverty. The restoration of accountability in the workplace through bargaining rights and guaranteed seats for workers on company boards, with full voting rights, should be the first step towards rebalancing power between employer and employee.

The freedom that capitalism relies on is a one-dimensional construct within a rigged system that absolves corporations from any liability save that of creating profit. Corporate law must be repurposed to take into account the need for businesses to recognise their social responsibilities. The rights of all stakeholders to share equally in profits should refocus remuneration away from executives and shareholders and towards workers and long-term investment. Governments must learn to work together on a global level, challenging the extractive model of capitalism and ensuring that taxes are paid in proportion to the profits made within each national jurisdiction. International cooperation is necessary to create a sustainable economy that respects the environment.

Transparency is the key to curbing the power of the tech giants. As artificial intelligence takes on a greater role in our homes, algorithms must be subject to regulatory oversight to ensure the decisions they make are free from bias. A digital bill of rights is needed to set an international framework protecting the personal data of individuals from misuse and exploitation without consent. Accountability must play a greater role in social media discourse, with sanctions for those who post abusive content.

There was once a different way of doing things. Progressive taxation helped narrow inequality and reciprocal obligations led to the provision of free health care, affordable housing and lifetime learning for those who sought it. Regulatory democracy kept the markets in check and greed wasn't good.

Now authoritarians and algorithms threaten democracy, while we argue over who has the right to speak. To protect ourselves from encroaching tyranny, we must look beyond a one-dimensional notion of what it means to be free and, by reconnecting liberty to equality and accountability, restore the individual agency engendered by the three dimensions of freedom.

References

p. 15: Donald Trump on political correctness
www.time.com/3988276/
republican-debate-primetime-transcript-full-text/

p. 24: Margaret Thatcher and *The Constitution of Liberty*
John Ranelagh, *Thatcher's People: An Insider's Account of the Politics, the Power and the Personalities* (HarperCollins, 1991)

p. 26: John Maynard Keynes: 'Let goods be homespun'
John Maynard Keynes, 'National Self-Sufficiency', *The Yale Review*, Vol. 22, no. 4 (June 1933)

p. 28: Reform of company law under Thatcher
'BoE's Haldane Says Corporations Putting Shareholders Before Economy', *Financial Times*, 25 July 2015

p. 29: Alan Greenspan: 'The world is governed by market forces'
Tages-Anzeiger, 19 September 2007

p. 31: The collapse of Carillion
'"Recklessness, hubris and greed" – Carillion slammed by MPs', *Guardian*, 16 May 2018

p. 49: Political correctness on US campuses
'The Rising Hegemony of the Politically Correct', *New York Times*, 28 October 1990

p. 53: Eric Weinstein and the Intellectual Dark Web
www.rebelwisdom.co.uk/8-posts/67-inside-the-intellectual-dark-web-with-eric-weinstein

p. 55: Ron Paul on 'cultural Marxism'
'Ron Paul Slams "Cultural Marxism" with a Quickly Deleted Bigoted Cartoon', *Reason*, 2 July 2018

p. 60: Safe-space rules for UK universities
Edinburgh University Students' Association Safe Space Policy:
www.eusa.ed.ac.uk/pageassets/eusapolicy/Edinburgh-University-Students-Association-Safe-Space-Policy(1).pdf

p. 62: Patriot Prayer in Portland, Oregon
www.truthout.org/articles/how-patriot-prayer-is-building-a-violent-far-right-movement-in-portland

p. 79: Tony Blair: 'rights and duties go hand in hand'
'My Vision for Britain: by Tony Blair', *Guardian*,
10 November 2002

p. 81: Michael Howard on the Human Rights Act
'Howard Attacks "Unfair" Rights Act', *Evening
Standard*, 18 March 2005

p. 82: EU regulation in the UK
www.theconversation.com/
is-eu-regulation-really-so-bad-for-the-uk-83193

p. 84: Vote Leave: 'we can't block EU laws'
www.voteleavetakecontrol.org/briefing_control.
html

p. 97: Free Trade vs climate change
www.desmog.co.uk/2018/08/09/economists-free-
trade-meet-independent-experts-ties-climate-
science-denial-pushing-no-deal-brexit

p. 99: Poll of English citizens on local
decision-making
www.bbc.co.uk/news/uk-england-44142843